The Secret Lives of Cats

The Secret Lives of Cats

A Collection of Poems
by
Thomas G. Payne

The Secret Lives of Cats
Copyright © 2011 by Thomas G. Payne

Illustrations by Mary Helene Sherman
Copyright © 2011 by Mary Helene Sherman

ISBN 978-0-9840185-0-5

Printed in the U.S.A. by CreateSpace

TGP Publishing
Laguna Beach, California

Please visit us at www.thomaspaynepoetry.com

Author's Notes

There is much to be learned about ourselves, about others, about our world, and about the meaning of life from the lives closest to us all. For many of us, our pets are very, very close. This book is dedicated to the many cats who were and still are very, very close to our family. From our family's collective memories, the following is a feline chronological history of the cats we all loved so much, and who inspired the deeper meaning of the stories and poems in *The Secret Lives of Cats.* .

First there was Pansie, as pretty as her namesake, who came to us in 1976 when our daughter Mary was about six years old. Mary's face would light up with glee and then love, after touching Pansie's grayish white fur. Pansie hid her first litter on the top shelf of the garage. Eventually she brought them, one by one, to our front door -- scratching and scratching until we finally opened it. There she stood with the first kitten dangling from her mouth. The rest soon followed.

Pansie's daughter, Pugsley, gave birth to Baby Pugs and Butch. They were as strong and robust as their mother, both white with grey and a touch of black. Frosty, our first white cat, was adopted from a box of kittens in front of the local market. Pugsley welcomed her in every way.

Black and white blended to create Sylvester, who we got from a litter given away by a lady in front of a local five-and-dime store. Sylvester became Sylvia when she ended up pregnant with Softy and Sneezy, who were bottle fed by my wife Mary Catherine.

They not only survived cat leukemia (which they caught from their mother) but both looked full grown by the time they were six months old!

Fluffy came to us from my dear Aunts Jean and Gen, in Ohio. Struck by a car she never heard, Fluffy was nursed back to health by my aunts, and sent to us air express. She was the sweetest cat we ever had and she got along with everyone. She died on Pacific Coast Highway. We realized after this sad incident that she must have been deaf. Later we learned that some white cats are, in fact, deaf.

Coco was our first Siamese, given to our daughter by our neighbor, Mary. In his former life he must have been a Samurai Warrior. He picked a fight with every cat in the neighborhood! Between fights he fathered our second Siamese, Coochie who, as a kitten, went all the way to San Francisco and back with us.

Coochie got pregnant by a neighbor's Persian named Fritzy. Fritzy was quite the fighter too. He produced some beautiful kittens. Coochie gave birth at Mary's, and her husband Joe's, house. In fact, she had four kittens on their bed at 4:00 a.m. Three were grey: Tipi, Baby, and Blue. The pure white one (who looked exactly like his father) came last. His name was Mondavi. Mondavi was as white as my best chardonnay. Tipi and Mondavi stayed with us and Blue and Baby went to live with grandma.

Percy "pig pen" was the smartest cat I ever knew – a wild cat who adopted us. She kept having litters because I could never catch her, until the day my daughter simply walked over and picked her up. Casper was simply a good friend, a close friend. He would greet me by standing on his hind legs like a dog, stretching his front legs on my thigh. Casper was stolen once, gone for two weeks, and found his way home. Casper and I twice stood side by side to fight off the meanest "Halloween" tomcat in our neighborhood. Casper was the best of the best for sixteen years.

Spooky was as pure black as her name implies. She gave birth to Belle, Blacky, and Charlie in our daughter's bathroom cabinet. Belle was mommy's girl and grew up so chubby she had to prop herself against a fence post to lick her belly. "Sweet Belle" we called her, though she was the deadliest predator for the 20 years she and Blacky lived with us. Charlie went to live at the Nun's convent. They had birds and rabbits and even a big dog that he got along with.

My wife and daughter found Laso at a local pet shop. Laso picked them out right away. Way too small to be separated from his mother, we became Laso's mom and dad. By six months old he had grown a mane, and we knew he was something special -- probably a Norwegian Forest cat. He was named for chasing his white tipped tail in a circular blur, like a lasso.

Fifteen years with Laso was just not enough. He was the love of our life. Laso never accepted Sassy, rescued at four-years-old, and adopted by my wife. She was the most beautiful of calicos. She fought for her place in our home, and remains with us to this day.

Laso and Sassy **are** The Secret Lives of Cats.

Words from Tom

Words are to be cherished, as they express one's thoughts and feelings that well up from the heart and soul. As a marketing consultant for nearly forty years, I have written millions of words of fact and educated opinion. But poetry is different. A poem sees life, sees the world in new ways that only the spirit can explain. The spirit of the cat world presented in this collection of poems is very real, as it not only came from my heart, but took place in our home. I am sure you will relate to the joys and the heartbreaks of being owned by your cats. I hope you will find the joy that these poems gave to me.

Thomas G. Payne

Original artwork by
Mary Helene Sherman

Contents

Why You Kiss a Cat

Do you kiss a cat because there is no one else to kiss,

    or

do you just like kissing furry heads
hiding very sharp teeth,

    or

do you love your cat more then you should?

    or

maybe you really, really love your cat,
when he purrrrrs for you.
Love and loneliness are like that.

As You

A balmy night of pristine dimension.
Quarter moon moves quickly, appearing,
now disappearing.
Precious Spooky tussles with her
rambunctious calico offspring.
Moist, still air wraps and bathes my skin.
Casper the cat leaps to my lap
seeking a tender scratch.
A night of comfort, a night of melancholy
reflective and introspective.
A time to recollect, serene.
Such nights have a fragrance,
a scent of the past, of you Mom,
and the old house at summer's ebb,
and tranquility secured.

I, the Cat

I am here, then I am gone.
I am here only to visit.
I take no commands unless
they suit my purposes.
I often disappear into my
world of smells, scents, and sounds,
of quick movements and intriguing shadows
that only my instincts can know.

I, the cat, first walked this
earth 50 million years ago.
I survive by a single purpose,
without reflection or self-doubt,
by stealth and strength, by
furtive skills and mercilessness.
I, the predator, attack without thinking.
I hear things before they happen.
I do not hesitate, nor do I consider.

I, the cat, act without the
thought of consequences.
I have no anxiety about the future.
Besides, I love my full food bowl,
and I love to purr.

The Whiskers on All of Us

The next time you look at your cat,
I'll bet you haven't noticed the whiskers.
Oh, you see the tiger marking and
the pretty pink nose, and those distinctive
and variegated colors of wildness, and
the white tipped paws hiding the claws of fierceness, and
the iridescent emerald eyes that cut through the dark and
seem to have no bottom.
But above all,
I believe cats are most proud of their whiskers,
that tells them, better than a sextant, where they can go.

I think a cat's whiskers are a lot like
the wrinkles around our eyes,
that say not only where you've been,
but where you have to go.

The Mended Heart

Melancholy is the color of her distant eyes,
eyes that weep from topaz to a deep sadness,
that quiet upwelling from fathomless longing.
For Sassy just wanted to be, just to be not alone.
Unlike human foster children,
Sassy's mother always wanted to be her mother.
But she could not keep her in this world where kittens
are but flesh and blood toys for amusement,
not brothers of sisters, and children of mothers.

After a long life as a foster child to many,
Sassy's separation turned to fear and her
loneliness turned to cowering and distrust.
Hiding herself away in a curled up fetal ball
with splotches of oranges and yellows, and
with delicate highlights of black Picasso shadows,
Sassy pulls her white fur coat over her shyness,
and trembles. For Sassy just wanted to be,
to be welcomed without conditions,
to find a place where her broken heart could mend.

That sunny Sunday summer morning we found her,
when the brilliance of the day shined so brightly
on Sassy's calico beauty and fate. Caged alone
and curled up behind the world of bars and her own fears,
in an auction place where togetherness is sold,

and where money buys only young and cute, there is
little market for five years of detachment and distress.

It has been four years now, and Sassy's topaz
eyes of melancholy have finally turned to belonging.
The closet no longer hides her and her fears.
Proud and accepted, Sassy stares down at you
in the bathtub, ready to splash down.
Adopted is a pair of green and white
polka-dotted sling-back sandals.
Of her day, much is spent perched
atop her pillow tuffet of our love.
At night she jumps into the lap, and only her lap,
the mother who saved her and allowed all of us into
Sassy's loving, mended heart.

For Mary Catherine

Such Things

I look at my cat Laso.
He's 14 and I'm 64.
So I guess we're about the same age.
And I wonder when he gets sick and in pain,
could I bear to put him to sleep?
But then I think, when the time comes
and all that I can feel is pain
and my mind has forgotten my soul,
such a kindness it would be to pass on into eternity.
After all, someone has to think about such things.

Why I Brush Laso

Nothing soothes Laso like a soft brush and a fine comb.
Brushing Laso, for these moments his call-of-the-wild nature
retreats into a rhythmic purr, and
those iridescent oval green eyes squint to smiling.
Claws retract and paws are tucked away.
This is when man and beast find communion.

Laso learned English a long time ago.
"Brush Laso," I call. Twenty pounds of Maine Coon cat
drops everything, and runs and jumps on my pool table, and
staring me right in the eye says, "It's about time,
breakfast is over, and you owe me a good brushing and
a fine combing because you've spoiled me- -
and besides I love to be brushed almost more
than pulling tails off of those tricky lizards.
You know this is the only time I'm going to be really,
really nice to you, but you still can't tell me what to do.
But I promise, no biting and no scratching- -
that is as long as you keep brushing. And don't stop!"

Why do I brush Laso??
I always do what I'm told.

Human Rights for All

It has been said,
that there are three conditions for having a soul —
    self-awareness,
            reason or intelligence, and
                    imagination.
These are the conditions,
ingredients, and the capacities
defining a sentient being.

It can be said,
that my cat, in fact all animals,
possess intelligence, especially to survive,
something we humans seem to have lost sight of.

As for self-awareness,
while my cat may not recognize himself in the mirror,
he is very aware of me, in relationship to himself,
following me everywhere around the house,
which, in itself, might make me question
a little of his intelligence.

As for imagination,
my cat often walks into our bedroom,
sees his favorite toy, which he knows is just a toy
by the power of his senses, far greater than mine, and
begins to play hide-and-go-hunt.

A game he imagined all by himself.
Therefore, I feel this qualifies as imagination,
especially considering that my left forearm has often
become an imagined toy, thus sending me
to the doctor's office on various occasions.

So what I'm getting at is that my cat,
and all of his close and distant relatives,
qualify as sentient beings, therefore having a soul,
and commanding the same --
(in our very unbalanced, unfair,
and often brutal world)
rights as us human beings.

Very soon my cat will finish and publish
his treatise "*On the Rights of and For
the Dignity of the Animal World.*"
I am truly hopeful that all of you out there
will support this long overdue addition to our Constitution.
After all, life, liberty, and the pursuit of happiness
is an inalienable right of all, and
my twenty pound Maine Coon cat means it!!!

Forgive

He didn't mean it,
That snap, that bite.
A reaction of instinct
Unplanned, without anger,
Without malice.

"No!" I yelled.
A snap
A small droplet of blood
Slowly
Trickled down my arm.
"No!" I yelled again.

Laso recoils.
I hurt his feelings.
He hurt me.
My arm stings.
Over in an instant
Forgotten
He purrs.

Of arms and blood,
Of cats and friends,
Forgive.

Sassy's Shoes

Her calico body,
a Peter Max splashing
of black, white, and orange.
Sassy sits and glows atop
a lady's size eight,
a sling back sandal,
polka dotted light green and white,
and scented by the caring feet
that carried her away out of that cage, and
into the light of our love.

Laso

He can see a gnat at 20 feet,
in a dark room,
this cat of mine,
who's supposed to be older,
in cat years, than me,
and still needs no glasses.
I wear my spectacles to make sure
I can see him purr.

Laso and Me

So glad am I
    to have had a 50-year head start
        on Laso my cat,
            so we can now grow old together.

Brushing Laso

"You know, Tom, I don't want
to seem arrogant or ungrateful,
and I certainly don't want to
come off like a know-it-all.
But, you have to admit we cats
have been around a lot longer than you folks.
Heck, we're the ones with history.
I've got relatives going back 50 million years.
Don't you get it? That's why you're
Always so amazed at how smart I am."

"Oh! That feels so good and keep brushing my back.
Okay, now do the top of my head.
Purrrrfect!"

"Another thing, Tom, you folks
haven't done such a good job
while you think you've been in charge.
You know, we're all on this earth together,
but you chop down my forests,
spill oil all over the place, and now
it's so bad I can hardly find a sparrow to munch on.
Then you turn my big cousins into
couture coats, and those gaudy belts,
and even stick your feet into those furry designer shoes."

"Okay now, I'm going to roll over a bit.
Now, brush my sides, and for this one time,
I'll let you brush my belly.
But just once!"

"And DO NOT touch my back feet,
strictly off limits!
Remember the last time you did that?
Well, I'm really sorry I bit your arm,
the doctor visit and the week of antibiotics.
Oh, don't forget to smooth out
My mane and tickle my chin."

"Anyway, as I was saying, Tom,
you folks haven't treated us very well,
but we come from a higher place.
I mean we never held a grudge."

"You guys get upset with each other
and bombs start falling,
you burn down your own towns,
start shooting at each other,
and protest in the streets.
Hey, have I or any of my relatives
hired an attorney, called the press,
formed picket lines, or joined the ACLU?
No!"

"Okay, okay, I know, brushing is about over.
Do you always have to give me that toothpaste?
And what's up with the new fur ball stuff?
You know I only like the fish flavor."

All done, Laso.

Unspoken

Music plays for two lives
furtively moving into old age,
one foot and then one paw in front of another.
Laso, he rests at my fingertips as always as I write.
Thoughts touching subject,
but my heart resting on his fur.
He gave up his wildness for me,
that prowess of instincts
and the lethal conquest of the kill.
For this, we are bound for always,
connected beyond the boundaries of our nature,
and intertwined eternally together
in a union of all life knowing living.

The Cat Without a Tail

The sun without his planets,
the earth without her sky,
the moon without her glow,
my father without his son,
ourselves without another,
my life without my love,
death without renewal,
a poem without a truth,
ice cream without the chill,
a wish without the come true,
a dog without a friend,
a hand without the fingers.
None of these can be worse than a cat without a tail.

Imagine Him

My Laso is a 20 pound Maine Coon cat.
He has a shiny back of long black fur
with a tinge of grey, and most spectacularly
a belly of white angora softer than chinchilla.
His tail, the lasso, is lengthy and tipped in white
as an artist might conceive, and a matching white chin
and neck regal only to his breed.
A curious, if not mysterious,
butterfly design drawn by his nature,
birthmarks the back of his neck,
just below the most beautiful face
and pinkest nose in God's Cat Kingdom.
A face held in a mane so full and so furry,
his whiskers had to grow enormously to
ensure a proper compass for his many adventures.

Now, if you can, imagine him,
this king of the domestic cat world 20 times larger.
Can you visualize the world's most
beautiful cat with the sweetest face
in the animal kingdom,
now the size of his lion and tiger cousins.
That's how big my heart is for him.
Imagine him.

That Tiny Heart

I see inside that tiny heart, a heart more important
than a universe of Big Bang creation,
derived from the cold, airless void
that never had a heart or cared.

In and by way of her tiny heart, this little life
creates a warmth and a glow more immense than our galaxy,
and radiates a power the great darkness could never give.
Maybe that is the secret to our lives, that despite
all of the trauma, the destruction, and
the death that surrounds us all, just a small
goodness wrung out of our daily existence
is still a light the great void could never switch on.

So this tiny heart, this little life, this calico cat
that now sleeps between my legs this night,
is in so many ways much bigger than the infinity of the cosmos,
where time measures not warmth, but only stillness, and
where endless expanse fails to fill a single life with caring.

Yes, we have each other,
for better or for worse,
and I have a cat who loves me always for the better.

There is a Lot to Learn

There is a lot to learn watching a cat, any cat,
but especially your cat, close up,
washing themselves, caring for themselves.
That long, pink, rough tongue
washing between each claw on each paw,
catching his protruding fur tufts between his teeth,
yanking, then licking the side of each paw
to a perfect clean, a saliva soap suds,
then washing alternatively his face,
first right and then left.
Cats must really love themselves.

Have you ever thought about loving yourself
enough to lick between your fingers and toes?
Maybe if we could, we would learn to love ourselves
a little more, maybe even to groom others instead
of taking a very impersonal shower,
then drying off with a very impersonal towel,
dressing, and then going back to our wars.

Laso
1995 – 2009

The Secret Lives of Cats
Sassy's Secret

Melancholy is the color of her distant eyes.
Sassy came into our hearts from a broken home,
torn away from her brother and left in a pet shop cage,
abandoned.
Five years old with no prospects,
my wife saw her and fell in love.
She was truly beautiful,
a calico cat with splotches of orange and yellow and red,
painted boldly on white,
with delicate highlights of black Picasso shadows.

But adjusting to our home would be difficult.
Sassy's sad past had turned to fear,
and her loneliness to distrust.
Then there was Laso, and this was his home!
Laso had come to live with us as an infant,
long before he should have been taken from his mother.
For Laso, this was not just his home, it was where he
grew up, and we were his father and mother.
There was no room in his heart,
in his domain for another.
Laso never considered Sassy more than a
foster child and an intruder. Laso was nine years old
when Sassy came to stay with us.
Sassy was not welcome.

Laso grew into his Maine Coon heritage,
all 20 pounds of him. He was gorgeous but menacing.
Black and grey silken fur showed with such brilliance.
But oh! that belly he used to entice our attention,
white angora with a big smile. Rough it up though,
and it became a Venus fly trap with big claws and sizeable fangs.

Years went by, five years; nothing worked.
Laso said no, and Sassy was afraid.
She had acclimated to her home and she was happy,
but shutter doors now separated our home
into "his" and "hers."
Spitting and cat screams,
hissing and paws banging our doors seemed to be
the sum total of their interaction.
Sassy became as determined as Laso.

Occasionally we monitored visitation in our kitchen
in the evening. Sassy stayed on her chair frozen in a cold stare,
and Laso showed his belly to entice her into his Venus fly trap.
These many kitchen sessions lasted several months,
with little success, before Laso's cancer showed up.
Strangely, after that discovery, I could swear something
different was happening between Sassy and Laso –
the long stare-you-down contests, and
an unusual level of high pitched noises and murmuring.
Catcalls? Talking? Cussing? Complaining?
Who knows? But something was up.

That Super Bowl evening Laso died.
Mary Catherine and I, and our daughter Mary
knew Laso's time with us was growing short.
But short never happened.
The end came with such agonizing thunder.
The end had come as now.
Fifteen years.

Fifteen years with Laso was just not enough.
I guess love always wants more.
Tears ran from our hearts for days.
We suffered, and it consumed our souls.
Our family had lost a son, a loved one.
But little did we know that when we rescued Sassy,
Sassy would rescue us!

It had been a week since Laso died.
Our house -- Laso's house -- was empty.
We still saw him everywhere,
these pictures that are our memories,
these hopes that he had never died,
we now cast our eyes away from.
But Laso was gone, and it was at just this darkest moment,
that Sassy said, "Laso told me, *tell them after I'm gone.*"
Sassy continued, "Laso and I, in the kitchen,
we talked all of the time.

You probably started to catch on that night
at the dinner table, just a few days before Laso left all of us.
He showed me his belly and,
of course, I pretended to ignore him.

That's when he said, *Tell them after I'm gone.*
So here's what he told me.

First Laso said, *Be especially nice to Tom,*
try to give him a little bit of your heart.
Even though you're a girl and you love
Mary Catherine more than anyone,
give Tom a little extra attention.
He and I have been as close as father and son
for nearly 15 years, and I wish not to break his heart.
So let him pick you up, put you on his lap for a while.
Lay next to him for a few minutes
when he watches T.V. on the floor, just like I did.
Sit next to him on his desk at night when he writes.
I'm sure he'll write another poem about you.
He'll even play music for you.
Oh, by the way, it's okay to walk and sit all over his papers,
he doesn't care.

Tom likes to comb and brush you,
he'll do it twice a day if you want him to,
and don't complain about the toothpaste
and the fur ball medicine.

Also, if you want, get Tom to open the back door
of his office at night.
There's all of those creepy-crawlers, weird sounds,
and my favorite, the crickets in the summer.

Now pay attention,
your best sun spot in the winter is on his desk, and in
the summer on the Chinese rug in the garden room.
Lastly, get Tom to give you water
out of the kitchen sink faucet, my favorite,
though this maybe a little unlady-like for you,
but Mary Catherine doesn't care.

Now, Mary Catherine is going to miss me a lot.
You should know she taught me everything
about how to act around the house,
and when I was good she kissed and kissed me
on the head, and squeezed me really tight.
So even though she has you,
swish her legs every morning at breakfast,
and every night at dinner, just like I did.
So Sassy, it's your house now,
so stop scratching the furniture — get some manners!

Now for little Mary. She is very sensitive and
emotional just like you,
so cut out the hissing, be sure to swish her
whenever she comes over, and please

watch your manners during yoga.
Don't forget to show them your belly just like this.

Sassy, since you'll have the run of the whole house now,
and you can sleep wherever you want, make sure you
still sleep on Mary Catherine's bed now and then.
Oh, and lastly, please leave the new floral arrangements alone.
I could never resist myself.
Those plants reminded me of when I lived outside,
and you remember the trouble I got into when
I got away every chance I got.

Now to you, Sassy, I know it's hard and not like you,
but don't scratch their friends when they come over to visit.
Strangers, well that's okay I guess, but not the friends.
And don't be a sissy when Tom and Mary Catherine
go for a trip. I've got them trained.
They're never gone long, and only sweet
Mary comes over, no strangers.
Also, you can have my favorite pillow to sleep on.
Even though it still smells like me and you might 'hissitate,'
it's really quite comfortable.

Sassy, I'm really sorry we didn't
get along for all of those years.
But you know I was here first, it was my house,
and Tom and Mary Catherine, and for that matter, Mary,
belonged to me.

But I do apologize for jumping you.
I know you never forgave me,
but gee whiz, couldn't you find one kind word for me?

But it all worked out, I got the upstairs and
Tom's office, and you got the downstairs and
Mary Catherine's softer than air king-sized bed.
But you should be more careful,
I heard you almost fell in the tub more than once.

Oh, you can have my catnip plant,
but lots of luck with the barf!

Well any way, that's about all I have to say.
You should know, just to make sure you're being good,
my cat spirit will be closely watching.
So, if you see a big, scary, dark shadow now and then,
don't be afraid -- it's just me.
So take care of Tom, Mary Catherine,
and little Mary, and have a 'purrrffectly'
wonderful life. I know I did.

                                    Love, Laso

Restfulness

My restless thoughts curled up against my belly,
warm, furry, and all fuzzy like my big cat Laso.
I reach down and pat his head,
but careful not to touch the sensitive belly,
not wanting to awaken the beast in me,
and have my thoughts kick me with those strong back feet,
or drive a fang of anxiety into my restfulness.

Laso said, " Don't take everything so seriously.
See how I have evolved. I'm just who I am, a cat.
Just accept who you are, your time and this place.
Now pet my head some more, and let your thoughts just purr,
and purr, and purr. Now Tom, see — isn't that better?"

A Gift

Let my hand be the morphine of your pain,
the hand that relieves your suffering
that you are unable to tell me about,
but that I wish to know.
Let my hand soothe your old age
as I hope another hand will comfort me.
I hear the music you play for me, and
drink the tears that well up in my gratitude -
all a small price for this joy and this wonderful sadness.

Going on Without You

I knew your time with me was growing short,
but short never happened.
The end, it came as now.
I spent your whole life with me,
but it was still not enough.
I guess that is the way of love.
Love always wants more and
gives more and cares more.
Love does not like short,
love likes forever.
But I now have memories and
they are all I have of you.
Like love, I want more.
But short memories of you,
they will never be.
They will be long and forever until
I will be but a memory,
loved like you, wanting more.

I love you Laso,
Tom

The Picture

I cast my eyes away from the picture that is my memory,
the image of you that is your suffering,
the vision of me as a helpless bystander
stroking your mane and caressing your head,
petting the luxury of the fine fur that is you,
speaking to console the trauma that is to be the death of you.
I cast my eyes away and you are gone.

More

I gave you all I could give you, and
all I want is to give you more.
But you are not here where my hand
can find the fine touch of you,
where I can kiss your head and
talk out loud of all of the thoughts
I have written tonight, and yesterday, and tomorrow.
This room is so empty now, visions,
my visions of you are but memories I place in front of me,
hoping they too give me back the more I want to give you.

My Cat Laso

He was part of me
part of my soul
for fifteen years.
When he left me,
when he died,
he ripped a hole in my soul
that will never grow back.

A Year After

It is not that I love you any less Laso,
this year for us gone by,
only that the pain has begun to fade
into the distant horizon of acceptance.

It is not that I love you any less
only that time has softened
the awful memory of the night you died.

It is not that I love you any less
only that the sorrow of missing you,
its grip upon my broken heart,
has relented a little upon me.

If there is to be a time after,
I know my joy of you will surely be as before,
and like the memory of the winter wind
ruffling the soft fur of your mane,
my longing for you will fade away when we meet again,
as my hand touches you, and the summer of our joy together,
begins again.

It is not that I love you any less, Laso,
I love you more.

A Small Palm

It took strength to sit here, pen in hand.
Lately, I have felt quite empty,
I guess you would say uninspired.
My thoughts have not hit me over the head,
no 2'x 4', not even a feather.
So I have begun to wonder why.
Maybe it has something to do with
a dream I had a while back.
My heart was saddened by this dream,
even though it could never be true,
that we let Laso,
our beautiful Maine coon cat of fifteen years,
go when he got sick with cancer,
and I ran and ran to find him,
to save him, to save me from terrible guilt,
and I found him, and he ran to me,
and I grabbed him and squeezed him,
and kissed him until I woke up.

So I've decided to visit his grave in our backyard.
I've been avoiding him for fear of more sadness –
that beautiful grave I dug and laid Laso down,
wrapped in his favorite blanket , along with
the baseball we use to play with –

his grave covered with white crushed rock
with a cobblestone border,
and now a small palm tree springing up between the rocks,
undoubtedly nourished by Laso's lovely, big essence.
I'm standing here now Laso, asking for some inspiration,
and then I look again at the small palm
and I know now Laso is trying to tell me,
"Get to work, Tom."
Yes, Laso, you know I always do what you tell me to.

One more goodbye to Laso from my daughter, Mary

Dear Laso,

It's Mary. I just wanted to share
how much I've missed you.
You were the beloved cat, but more.
You were my brother, my friend, my joy.
When you were a young boy I was crazy about you.
Remember our games of hide and seek?
That time I went to Italy for three whole weeks,
I couldn't wait to get back to you.

When I moved out of the house,
I went and got my very own cat.
As much as I loved him and still do,
you were the one I loved and still love the most.

You were fun when you were young
and grand when you were old.
You brought so much happiness to my life
as I know I did to yours.
The way you could gaze with those big emerald eyes!
You were and still are a treasure.

I loved the way your face would light up
whenever you saw me. I loved how you would
hobble from one room into the kitchen just to see me.
As you got older I know that could be hard for you,
but you did it because you loved me.

The day before you died, I told you, with tears
running down my face, how much I truly loved you.
I hope you heard me, Laso.
And on the evening that you died, you held
your head up high and gazed into my eyes.
You held onto my gaze as if to say
how much you loved me.

I'm sorry you are gone, but I am more grateful
that you were my brother, my friend and my joy.

You were the best cat that ever lived, Laso.
The best brother a girl could ever want.

Someday I hope to see you again.
Until then chase the lizards and
stay away from the skunks.

> Love always,
> Your sister, Mary

About the Author

Mr. Payne, a real estate marketing consultant for nearly forty years, has been blessed with a life-long passion for reading and writing poetry. While he has written millions of words of fact and educated opinion, his poetry "sees life, sees the world in new ways that only the spirit can explain." Having put pen to paper for many years and with urging from friends, family and book store owners, he decided it was time to organize his body of work into a series of collections for publication. This first collection pays homage to the joy and heartbreak of "being owned by your cats" and allows access to some of their secrets.

TGP Publishing
Laguna Beach, California

Please visit us at www.thomaspaynepoetry.com